ALONG THE SANTA FE TRAIL

MARION RUSSELL'S OWN STORY

By Marion Russell
Adapted by Ginger Wadsworth
Illustrated by James Watling

ALBERT WHITMAN & COMPANY • MORTON GROVE, ILLINOIS

FOR MARK AND DAN,
TRAILBLAZERS INTO THE TWENTY-FIRST CENTURY. G.W.

FOR SIMEON. J.W.

Photo of Marion Russell on page 40 is courtesy
of the Pueblo Library District, Pueblo, Colorado.

The text of this book is set in Janson.
The illustrations are rendered in colored ink and colored pencil.
Design by Karen Johnson Campbell.

Text copyright ©1993 by Ginger Wadsworth.
Illustrations copyright ©1993 by James Watling.
Published in 1993 by Albert Whitman & Company,
6340 Oakton Street, Morton Grove, Illinois 60053-2723.
Published simultaneously in Canada by
General Publishing, Limited, Toronto.
Printed in the United States of America.
10 9 8 7 6 5 4 3 2 1

Russell, Marion Sloan, 1845–1936.
Along the Santa Fe Trail: Marion Russell's own story /
Marion Russell; adapted by Ginger Wadsworth;
illustrated by James Watling.
p.   cm.
Summary: In 1852, seven-year-old Marion Sloan Russell travels
with her mother and older brother in a wagon train along the
Santa Fe Trail, experiencing both hardship and wonder.
ISBN 0-8075-0295-2
I. Russell, Marion Sloan, 1845–1936—Juvenile literature.
[1. Santa Fe Trail—Juvenile literature. 2. Frontier and
pioneer life—Southwest, New—Juvenile literature.
3. Overland journeys to the Pacific—Juvenile literature.]
II. Wadsworth, Ginger. III. Watling, James, ill.
IV. Title.
F786.R96 1993   93-6491
917.8—dc20   CIP
                                                  AC

When she was in her eighties, Marion Sloan Russell began telling her daughter-in-law, Winnie McGuire Russell, the adventures of her life. Winnie Russell wrote down Marion's words, and Marion read and corrected the work. It was published as Land of Enchantment: Memoirs of Marian Russell along the Santa Fe Trail.

Marion Russell was born on January 26, 1845, in Peoria, Illinois. Over her lifetime she was to travel back and forth five times on the Santa Fe Trail, which began in Independence, Missouri, and extended almost eight hundred miles to Santa Fe, New Mexico. The trail was primarily an important trade route, and later, a mail and stagecoach route as well. More than five thousand wagons a year used the trail by the late 1860s; by 1880, the railroad had reached Santa Fe, and travel by wagon was no longer necessary.

Marion's memoirs reflect the perspective of white settlers. However, later in her memoirs, she does wonder about the Indians "who watched with bitter eyes that vast migration" across their land. Some Native Americans were understandably hostile as they saw white settlers kill buffalo and claim their homelands.

My story is adapted from Marion Russell's text. I had wanted to write my own version of her first trip on the Santa Fe Trail. Then I realized that my words seemed flat in comparison to Marion's eloquent voice. I returned to her memoirs and used her words as much as possible. In a few places I added transitions or altered phrases so the story would flow smoothly. My version of her first trip is shorter, but the essence of the story is Marion's, in both words and spirit.

For an unknown reason, Marion's name in the original memoirs is spelled Marian. But in family papers and on her tombstone, the spelling is Marion, which I have used.

Ginger Wadsworth

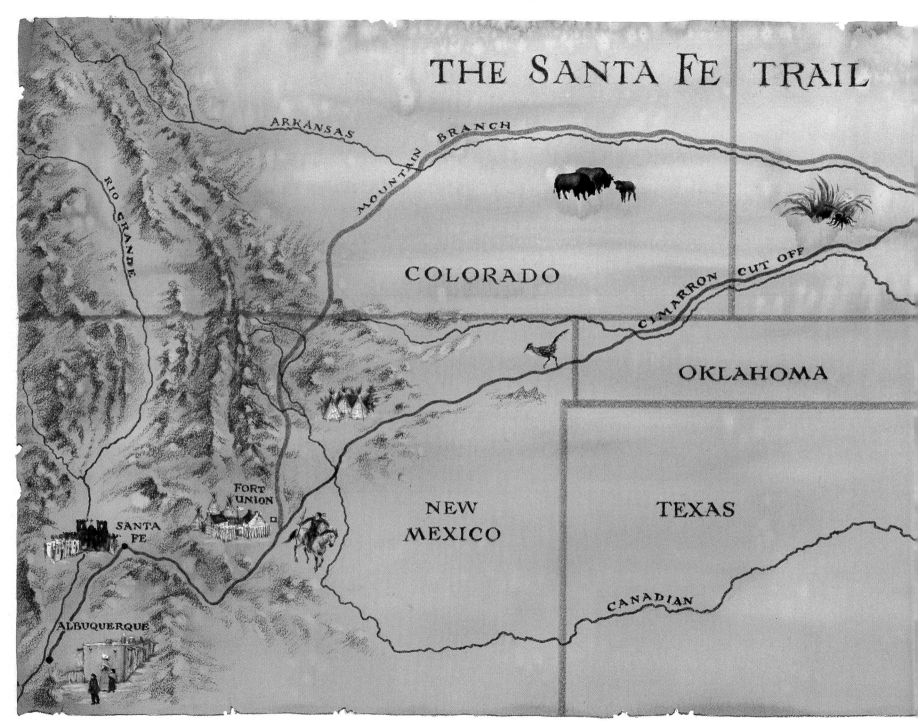

The red line traces the route Marion Russell, her mother, and brother traveled in 1852.

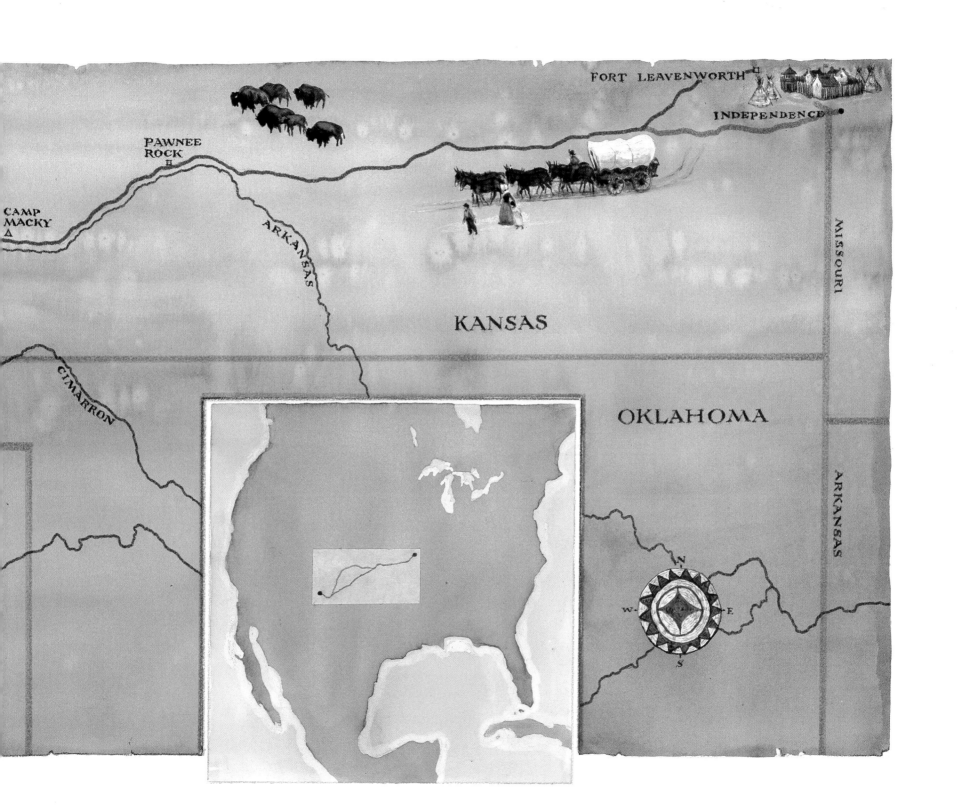

FORT LEAVENWORTH

INDEPENDENCE

PAWNEE
ROCK

CAMP
MACKY

ARKANSAS

KANSAS

MISSOURI

CIMARRON

OKLAHOMA

ARKANSAS

N
W E
S

My stepfather, Mr. Mahoney, was an experienced scout, but he was killed by the Indians while on a scouting expedition on the prairies. I remember mostly my mother and how, when the news came, she leaned against the wall for support, one hand clutching at her throat as if she were choking. I remember the horror in her eyes.

After my stepfather's death, Mother, Will, and I waited two long years in Kansas City for Grandfather to come from California and take us there. He said we might wash out much gold if we cared to. But we waited in vain. That was the year of the cholera epidemic, and Grandfather and both of his sons died in it and were buried in faraway California.

When school closed in the spring of 1852, Mother decided that we would go to California anyway. So we moved to Fort Leavenworth in Kansas, where emigrant trains prepared to travel west. Mother had planned that we were to take passage in Captain Francis Xavier Aubry's train, for some of the Indians were hostile along the Santa Fe Trail, and she had great confidence in him. Two army officers and a doctor offered Mother, Will, and me transportation as far as Fort Union in New Mexico Territory if mother would prepare their meals en route for them. Mother agreed. She saved the five-hundred-dollar fare by cooking for the young men.

The dread cholera was raging in Fort Leavenworth the October day our white-hooded wagons set sail on the western prairies. Captain Aubry broke camp first; his great wagon swayed out onto the trail. We heard his powerful voice

calling orders to follow. Wagon after wagon rolled onward; the train numbered five hundred wagons. Tar barrels were burning in the streets to ward off the cholera, and clouds of black smoke drifted over us as we pulled out.

After a few days on the trail, we settled into a familiar pattern. Each morning the camp was astir at daybreak. Men began rolling out from under the wagons where they had been sleeping. They stood up in the cold morning air to stretch their arms and to rub their eyes. Through partially closed tent flaps and wagon curtains, women could be seen slipping their dresses over their heads. I found it hard to button all the buttons that ran up and down the back of my dress. Why couldn't they have been put in front where I could get at them? Will sometimes helped me, for Mother was busy cooking.

Dressed and out in the sunshine, we were all happy. Sunbonnets bobbed merrily over cooking fires, and a smell of coffee was on the air. Packing was done swiftly, and the mules hitched to the wagons. Then the children were counted and loaded. Drivers called, "Get up there! Come along, boys!" Whips cracked, and all about the heavy wagons began groaning. The mules leaned into the collar, and the great wheels began their steady creaking.

The man in charge of our wagon was a Frenchman called Pierre. He almost always walked, but at times he sat swinging his booted feet over the dashboard—perilously close to the brown mules' swinging hips. Sometimes he sang or talked in French to the mules. His limp black hat turned straight up in front. His blue shirt was dotted thickly with little white stars. His dark eyes were like a hawk's eyes, and his nose was like a beak.

Will, who was nine, usually walked with Pierre. He tanned in the sun, and there seemed boundless energy in his slender body.

Mother sat erect on the spring seat, her face rosy in the depth of her bonnet. Frequently she knitted as we bumped along, and often as meal and camp time drew near, she sat there and peeled potatoes.

Our food and cooking things were kept in a great box at the rear of the wagon. Two blackened kettles and a water pail hung from the running gear.

I was seven on this trip, and I could not keep up with Will and Pierre.
Often, when I got tired, I would crawl back among the blankets where I would
play with my doll or fall asleep.

Each noon we would halt for a brief hour's rest. The lunch was a cold one.
The mules fed on the crisp buffalo grass while the drivers rested. I remember the

tired men lying under the shade of the wagons, their hats covering their faces
as they slept. I can see the tired, sweaty mules rolling over and over in the grass,
delighted to be free from the heavy wagons.

After the noon rest, we would go on again, until the sun was low in the West.

The vast open country that is gone from us forever rippled like a silver sea in the sunshine. Running across that sea of grass were the buffalo trails—narrow paths worn deep into the earth. They were seldom more than eight inches across and always ran north and south. A buffalo is a wise animal. It knows instinctively that water flows eastward away from the Rocky Mountains and that the nearest way to running water is always north or south.

Scattered along the buffalo trails were the buffalo wallows, small lagoons of rainwater like turquoise beads strung on a dark-brown string. They were made by buffalo bulls fighting. The bulls would put their heads together and slowly walk round and round, making a depression that caught the rainwater.

Always there were buffalo. Our trail often led among herds of buffalo so numerous that at times we were half-afraid.

Frightening thunderstorms came up suddenly. The drivers would wheel the wagons so that the mules' backs were to the storm. The men who had been walking sought shelter with the women and children inside. The prairies would darken, and a sheet of drenching water would fall from the skies upon us. A fine white mist would come through the tightened canvas, and soon small pearls glistened in Mother's hair. Then, as suddenly as it had come, the storm would pass away.

We would emerge then from the wagons to stretch our cramped limbs. Always we saw our storm, a tattered beggar, limping off across the distant hills.

One evening a great rainbow flashed through the sunlit rain. I called out to Mother, who stood on the wagon tongue. Will, who was busy kindling a cooking fire, said with some eloquence, "There is always a pot of gold at the end of each rainbow."

"Mother, is it really true about the pot of gold?" I asked.

Mother smiled. "The end of the rainbow is always much farther away than it seems, dear. We can only follow the rainbow and hope that it leads to fame and fortune."

For years I thought that the end of the rainbow was in California.

At sunset the prairie sky flared into unbelievable beauty, with long streamers of red and gold flung out across it. Each night there were two great circles of wagons. Inside each great circle the mules were turned after grazing, for ropes were stretched between the wagons and a circular corral made. The cooking fires were inside the corral.

Between the two night circles formed by the wagons was a no-man's land which the children used as a playground. The ball games that went on there, the games of leapfrog and dare base!

And sometimes, far away, we heard the war whoop of the Indians. Men stood on guard each night, rifles in hand. They circled and recircled the big corrals.

After the evening meal, we would gather around the little fires. The men would tell stories of the strange new land before us, tales of gold and of Indians.

One night when the wind was blowing, Captain Aubry came and held me on his lap. I felt the great, black night closing down upon us and heard the voice of the night wind as it swept across the turbulent prairie. I shivered in the Captain's arms, thinking that only in the circle of the firelight that flickered on Mother's face was there warmth and comfort and home.

While most of the drivers slept under the wagons, the women and children slept inside the wagons or in tents. Each night we pitched our tent close to the wagon, and it spread its dark wings over the three of us. It was easy to hear Pierre snoring outside. Our bed on the matted grass was comfortable, but sometimes in the night I would awaken to hear the coyote's eerie cry in the darkness. Then I would creep close to Mother.

Our long caravan, loaded with heavy, valuable merchandise to be sold in the West, traveled slowly. Sometimes we were alarmed by the Indians, sometimes we were threatened by storms, and always it seemed we suffered for want of water.

I remember so clearly the beauty of the earth, and how, as we bore westward, the deer and the antelope bounded away from us. There were miles and miles of buffalo grass, blue lagoons, and blood-red sunsets, and once in a while, on the lonely prairie, a little sod house—the home of some hunter or trapper.

We paused at Pawnee Rock and Camp Macky; then we moved on.

Babies were born as our wagons lumbered westward.

Death sometimes came.

After about a month, we were on the Cimarron Cutoff. We built our fires with buffalo chips. My chore was to gather the chips. I would stand back and kick them, then reach down and gather them carefully, for underneath lived big spiders and centipedes. Sometimes scorpions ran out. I would fill my long, full skirt with the evening's fuel and take it back to Mother.

It was on this trip that I made my first acquaintance with the big, hairy spider called a tarantula. They lived in holes in the ground. When we found such a hole, we would stamp on the ground and say, "Tarantula, Tarantula! Come out, come out! Tell us what it is all about." And sure enough they would come out, walking on stiltlike legs.

As we continued in a southwesterly direction, there was less and less forage for our mules and horses. We found rattlesnakes and a variety of cactus that resembled trees.

Sometimes little jeweled lizards would dart across our path. Birds with long tails would walk the trail before us. The drivers called them roadrunners.

Once we traveled for two whole days without water, and thirsty child though I was, I felt sorrier for the straining mules than for myself. Captain Aubry told us how the muddy water in the buffalo wallows had often saved human lives. "One dying of thirst," he said, "does not stop for gnats or impurities."

Mother, Will, and I had to wash our faces and hands in the same basin of water. Will washed last, for Mother said he was the dirtiest.

After we had traveled for what seemed like an eternity across the hot, dry land, we awoke one morning to find the air filled with a cool, misty rain, which lasted all day. In the late afternoon we reached a flat mesa. There were a dozen Indian lodges there, and we saw smoke issuing from the tops. We saw Indian children slither through the wet drizzle among the stunted cedar trees and the lodges. Somehow it seemed we had entered a strange land of enchantment. This was different from anything we had seen.

Captain Aubry told us we were now in New Mexico Territory. "This is the land," he said, "where only the brave or criminal come. But it is a land that has brought healing to the hearts of many. There is something in the air of New Mexico that makes the blood red, the heart to beat high, and the eyes to look upward. Folks don't come here to die—they come to live, and they get what they come for."

We were a bit over two months reaching Fort Union in New Mexico.
There, our great cavalcade rested.

The tired mules were turned out to graze on the prairies. Freight was
unloaded, and two hundred horses turned into the corral. Army officers perched
on the fence to look over and choose their horses. The ground was a shambles

of buffalo hides, Mexican blankets, and sheep pelts—things to be sent back east.

Our camp was outside the Fort Union gate that stood open, and all day Will and I came and went as we pleased. Two friendly Indians sat and played mumblety-peg on a spread blanket. Will joined them and lost all his marbles.

When the mules had rested, we struck the westward trail again, starting out on a cold December morning. We were in Santa Fe before we knew it. We passed through a great wooden gateway that arched high above us. We moved along narrow alleylike streets past iron-barred windows. We saw a church with two cupolas. We saw old adobe walls and strings of red peppers drying.

Our caravan wiggled through donkeys, goats, and chickens. We came to a plaza where a tall man with a gun told us where to go. Dogs barked at us. Big-eyed children stared at us; shawled women smiled shyly.

As darkness deepened, there was a great hunting for clean shirts and handkerchiefs. Pierre even drew the comb through his choppy mustache. From the dance hall came the tinkle of guitar and mandolin—a *baile* was forming. We slept in the wagon, or tried to, but the noise and confusion kept us awake. Pierre had gone to the dance, and it was hard to sleep without the sound of his snores near us.

In a few days, we continued our long trek to California. One evening as the wagon train drew near to Albuquerque, New Mexico, Mother discovered that a small workbasket in which she kept her money and jewels was gone.

Some of the jewelry was found, but no part of the money was ever discovered. I was too young to realize what the loss of the money meant to my mother, but I do remember the shadow that settled on her bright face as we journeyed on. Now she did not have enough money to pay for the rest of our passage. When we reached Albuquerque, we had to leave the train that was to have carried us to the gold fields of California.

Will and I went house hunting with her. I remember the tears that rolled down her face as she sold a great yellow brooch and a pair of earrings. She rented an old adobe house on the outskirts of Albuquerque and began taking in boarders.

I remember the morning Pierre carried our luggage into the mud house. He tried to say something, but his mustache only wiggled. Mother tried to speak, too, but as usual when she was stirred deeply, she was silent, pressing her hand to her throat as if choking.

Will and I stood in the bare, windswept yard, watching the long wagon train pull westward. When we turned back, our surroundings seemed desolate.

There was no looking back. We were soon busy cleaning and whitewashing our little adobe, not knowing then how many mud palaces were to be ours in the future, or that in time we would come to love them. When I grew up, I said to myself, I would travel endlessly back and forth over the Santa Fe Trail. I loved the trail and would always live on it. These were the dreams of my childhood.

When Marion Russell was nine, Captain Aubry was stabbed to death in Santa Fe during a quarrel.

A few years later, when the Civil War started, Will joined the Union Army. Marion and her mother, Eliza Mahoney, didn't see him again for fifty years. Following the war, he was ordained a Baptist minister. He became a missionary in Calcutta, India, then a minister in Mexico City, and eventually returned to the United States. In 1917, Will was buried near Fort Leavenworth, Kansas, where he, Marion, and their mother had departed with Captain Aubry's wagon train in 1852.

Marion's mother did not remarry. She went back and forth over the Santa Fe Trail many times. As Marion recounts, "She was never quite happy unless she was passing back and forth over it...or planning to." She at last traveled to California, and died of old age in Los Angeles.

Marion traveled again and again on the Santa Fe Trail, first with her mother and brother, and then with her husband. She met Lieutenant Richard D. Russell at Fort Union when she was nineteen. They married the following year, in 1865. After the Civil War, they settled in Trinidad, Colorado, to raise their family.

Marion and Richard Russell had nine children, sixteen grandchildren, twenty-two great-grandchildren, and four great-great-grandchildren. Marion died in 1936 at the age of ninety-one, after being struck by an automobile. She was buried beside her soldier husband.

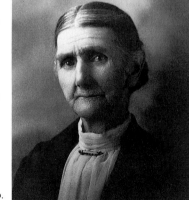

Marion Russell, about 1910.